Sports

I Can Skateboard

By Edana Eckart

Welcome Books™

Children's Press®
A Division of Scholastic Inc.
New York / Toronto / London / Auckland / Sydney
Mexico City / New Delhi / Hong Kong
Danbury, Connecticut

Photo Credits: Cover and all photos by Maura B. McConnell
Contributing Editor: Jennifer Silate
Book Design: Mindy Liu

Library of Congress Cataloging-in-Publication Data

Eckart, Edana.
  I can skateboard / by Edana Eckart.
    p. cm. — (Sports)
  Summary: Photographs and simple text show the steps involved in learning
  to skateboard.
  Includes bibliograhical references (p.) and index.
  ISBN 0-516-24278-4 (lib. bdg.) — ISBN 0-516-24370-5 (pbk.)
  1. Skateboarding—Juvenile literature. [1. Skateboarding.] I. Title.

GV859.8 .E37 2003
796.22—dc21
                                                            2002011314

Contents

My name is Erin.

I am going to **skateboard**.

4

I put on a **helmet** before
I skateboard.

It will keep my head safe
if I fall.

I put **pads** on my knees.

I also put pads on my elbows.

The pads will keep me safe.

9

This is my skateboard.

It has four wheels.

11

First, I put one foot on the skateboard.

I push on the ground with my other foot to move forward.

13

I stand **sideways** on my skateboard.

I am skateboarding!

14

I bend my knees.

I also put my arms out to my sides.

I am **careful** not to fall.

16

17

Now, I must turn left.

I **lean** to my left.

18

19

I am going to skateboard all day!

New Words

careful (**kair**-fuhl) to pay close attention

helmet (**hel**-mit) a hard hat that protects your head during sports or dangerous activities

lean (**leen**) to bend toward or over something

pads (**padz**) soft materials used to provide protection

sideways (**side**-wayz) toward one side

skateboard (**skate**-bord) a small board with wheels that you stand on and ride; to ride on a skateboard

To Find Out More

Books
Skateboarding in Action
by Bobbie Kalman
Crabtree Publishing

Skateboards: Designs and Equipment
by B. A. Hoena
Capstone Press

Web Site
Board World
http://library.thinkquest.org/J002968/
This Web site has information about skateboarding history, stars, and equipment.

Index

About the Author
Edana Eckart has written several children's books. She enjoys bike riding with her family.

Reading Consultants
Kris Flynn, Coordinator, Small School District Literacy, The San Diego County Office of Education

Shelly Forys, Certified Reading Recovery Specialist, W.J. Zahnow Elementary School, Waterloo, IL

Sue McAdams, Former President of the North Texas Reading Council of the IRA, and Early Literacy Consultant, Dallas, TX